INTERVIEWING PERPETRATORS OF RACIAL HARASSMENT

Gerard Lemos has been a consultant and trainer on race and equal opportunities since 1989, after being the Director of ASRA Greater London Housing Association and holding various senior management jobs at Circle 33 Housing Trust in London. Since then he has worked as a consultant for both housing associations and local authorities, as well as with the Housing Corporation and the National Federation of Housing Associations.

Gerard Lemos also advises and trains in public and private sector organisations outside the housing field. He is the author of several books related to race and equal opportunities which are to be published by the National Federation of Housing Associations.

INTERVIEWING PERPETRATORS OF RACIAL HARASSMENT

A guide for housing managers

Gerard Lemos

LEMOS ASSOCIATES
LONDON

Published in Great Britain 1993 by

Lemos Associates
82 Dartmouth Park Hill
London N19 5HU

Telephone 071 263 2306

© Lemos Associates 1993

ISBN 1-898001-00-6

A CIP catalogue record for this book is
available from the British Library

Designed by Mick Keates
Phototypeset by Kerrypress Ltd, Luton
Printed by BPCC Wheatons, Exeter

CONTENTS

INTRODUCTION

What is racial harassment?

'The most shameful and dispiriting aspect of race relations in Britain is the incidence of racial attacks and harassment.'[1] This is the view of the House of Commons Home Affairs Committee. Incidents during the late 1980s and early 1990s in France and Germany demonstrate that Britain is not alone in facing this problem; but it would be dangerous to allow the view to grow that racial harassment is exclusively the consequence of far right activity and so not a matter of concern in this country. Racial harassment has been defined by the Commission for Racial Equality as

> Violence which may be verbal or physical and which includes attacks on property as well as on the person, suffered by individuals or groups because

---

1. Home Affairs Committee (Third Report), *Racial Attacks and Harassment*, House of Commons, HMSO 1986, p.iv.

of their colour, race, nationality or ethnic or national origins, when the victim believes that the perpetrator was acting on racial grounds, or there is evidence of racism.[2]

Racial harassment can start with verbal abuse and sometimes escalates to criminal damage and assault. The catalogue of types of incidents that frequently occur is depressing and distressing. The former Greater London Council's (GLC) race and housing action team noted the following in 1985:

> racist name-calling, rubbish, rotten eggs, rotten tomatoes, excreta, etc., dumped in front of victims' doors, urinating through the letter box of victims, fireworks, burning materials and excreta pushed through the letter box, door-knocking, cutting telephone wires, kicking, punching and spitting at victims, serious physical assault, damage to property, e.g., windows being broken, doors smashed, racist graffiti daubed on floors and walls. Dogs, cars and motorcycles are still being used to frighten black people. Shotguns and knives have also been used occasionally.[3]

In some very extreme cases the result of racial harassment is death. Amongst others, the Khan family of Walthamstow, London in 1981[4] and the Kassan

---

2. Commission for Racial Equality, *Living in Terror: A Report on Racial Violence and Harassment in Housing*, CRE, 1987, p.8.
3. Report (14 February 1985) by Head of Housing Services, GLC (TH192), p.2, referred to in Third Report of Home Affairs Committee.
4. *Living in Terror*, p.10.

family of Ilford, Essex in 1985 were the victims of fatal arson attacks.[5] In December 1991 Panchadcharam Sahitharan, a Tamil refugee, was ambushed and battered to death with sticks and baseball bats.[6] In August 1992 Ruhulla Aramesh was beaten to death with an iron bar by a gang of about 15 youths who broke down his front door in Croydon, south London.[7]

The national picture

Whilst the documented evidence is more extensive in some areas, and there is little doubt that the problem is significantly more frequent and severe in areas such as Tower Hamlets and Newham, researchers for the Runnymede Trust concluded in 1986:

> Few areas in Britain can now be regarded as safe for black residents . . . racial attacks have taken place in areas such as middle-class Hendon, in Finchley and in Shrewsbury in rural Shropshire.[8]

Home Office figures show a steady rise since the mid 1980s to 8,000 reported incidents in 1991.[9] A committee of Members of the European Parliament put the figure at about 70,000 in 1991.[10]

In Glasgow, an area 'not noted for racial strife' in the view of the Home Affairs Committee, of a group of 50

---

5. Ibid, p.42.
6. *The Independent*, 27 October 1992.
7. *The Independent*, 9 November 1992.
8. *Racial Violence and Harassment*, Runnymede Trust 1986, p.15.
9. *The Independent* 9 November 1992.
10. Ibid.

Asian families 40 per cent of the Pakistanis and 58 per cent of the Indians had experienced physical attacks; 48 per cent and 41 per cent respectively, damage to property; 52 per cent and 54 per cent respectively, racist graffiti on their homes, and 88 per cent and 100 per cent respectively, racial abuse.[11]

Even the relatively small Asian community in Edinburgh reported 35 racially motivated incidents between January 1985 and April 1986.[12]

Reported racial attacks and harassment in the Metropolitan Police area in 1991 totalled 3,169 incidents. This has risen from a total of 1,877 in 1985.[13] In his annual report for 1991 the Commissioner commented, 'It would be wrong to interpret these figures as showing an increase in racial attacks. I believe they show an increased willingness to come forward and report these incidents to police.'[14] The Commissioner's belief may be right, though clearly difficult to prove. It is not, however, a universally held opinion.

The London Borough of Newham's study in 1986 found that one in four of Newham's black residents had been victims of some form of racial harassment in the previous year. Two out of three had been victims more than once, and 116 victims reported 1,550 incidents of racial harassment. These included 774 cases of insulting behaviour, 188 cases of attempted damage to property, 175 cases of attempted theft, 174 cases of threats of

---

11. Third Report of Home Affairs Committee, app.7, p.53.
12. Third Report of Home Affairs Committee, app.7, p.55–56.
13. Annual Report of The Commissioner of Police of the Metropolis, 1991.
14. Ibid.

damage or violence, 153 cases of physical assault, and 40 cases of damage to property.[15]

In Tower Hamlets, one list of 495 racial incidents included 15 of arson or attempted arson, 94 of criminal damage, 61 of assault causing injury, 181 of verbal threats and abuse, 32 of stone throwing and 102 of banging and kicking on doors.[16]

The Greenwich Action Committee Against Racial Attacks has recorded more than 200 racist incidents in the year to October 1992. Of these, 177 assaults were against women.[17]

Who is racially harassed?

It is not solely black and ethnic minority people who are harassed on the grounds of their race; however, the evidence points clearly to the fact that they are overwhelmingly the victims. In the statistics of the Metropolitan Police, out of a total of 3,169 racially motivated incidents reported to them in 1991, 1,783 were against Indian or Pakistani people, and 639 were against African or Afro-Caribbean people. In other words, more than 80 per cent of attacks were against black people.[18]

On the Teviot housing estate in east London, one third of 323 racist attacks recorded in a twelve month period were directed at refugees, mostly Somalis.[19]

---

15. *Living in Terror*, p.9.
16. Third Report of the Home Affairs Committee, p.iv.
17. *The Independent*, 9 November 1992.
18. Annual Report of the Commissioner of Police of the Metropolis.
19. *The Independent*, 9 November 1992.

Who are the perpetrators?

The perpetrators are not exclusively white; however, 'the typical perpetrator is a white teenager, often part of a gang and sometimes encouraged by parents.'[20]

In October 1992 Birmingham City Council was granted possession against a white couple whose sixteen-year-old son racially abused and attacked a Punjabi woman neighbour for two years. In granting possession against the parents the judge commented, 'Having heard the evidence and seen the witnesses I believe the son is beyond his parents' control'.[21] In situations such as this one, the tenants (in this case the parents) are generally responsible for any breaches of the tenancy agreement by their children under the age of 18 who are resident in the property, hence the granting of possession.

The Policy Studies Institute (PSI) survey in 1984, commenting principally on attacks in the street, noted that 'a large proportion of these attacks are by gangs of youths, often identified as "skinheads". Eight of the black victims specifically mentioned "skinheads", and a further eight mentioned gangs of young white people who attacked them in the street.'[22] It should be stressed, however, that the incidents already mentioned were by no means exclusively perpetrated by 'skinheads'.

---

20. Third Report of the Home Affairs Committee, p.v.
21. *The Independent*, 27 October 1992.
22. *Black and White Britain: The third PSI survey*, Heinemann 1984, p.255.

What needs to be done?

The reported incidence of racial harassment against black and ethnic minority people continues to grow, either because reporting is increasing, or the problem is getting worse; it is likely that both reasons contribute to the rise. The onus is therefore now on social housing organisations to support victims sensitively and to deal with perpetrators effectively. So, many organisations have taken three essential steps. Firstly, they have made racial harassment a ground for seeking possession under their tenancy agreement.[23] Secondly, they have adopted policies and procedures for dealing with racial harassment, sometimes along with other forms of harassment. Thirdly, they have arranged training for their staff.

It is clear that the problem is not susceptible to simple solutions; some of the approaches being set out in policies may have good intentions, but are difficult to implement in practice. Uncountenanced obstacles occur, or the case is too particular and enigmatic to be handled within the boundaries of a logical and occasionally inflexible policy.

Sometimes the attitudes and behaviour of housing staff interrupt their ability to see a situation objectively

---

23. The standard wording suggested by the National Federation of Housing Associations in its recommended form of assured tenancy is: 'The tenant agrees not to commit or allow members of his/her household or invited visitors to commit any form of harassment on the grounds of race, colour, religion, sex, sexual orientation or disability which may interfere with the peace and comfort of, or cause offence to, any other tenant, member of his/her household, visitors or neighbours.'

and to communicate clearly with both perpetrator and victim. This is not always because they deny the experience of, or lack sympathy for, victims of racial harassment. It can be because their own strong condemnation of racism in all its forms means that the legally constrained and pragmatic choices on offer feel frustrating and unsatisfactory – feelings often shared by their managers, not to mention the victims themselves.

In some cases the perpetrator will not have been identified. The priority has then to be support for the victim. In other cases the perpetrator may be known but not be a tenant of the same landlord as the victim. In either of those circumstances different strategies will be necessary to the ones in this guide. The approaches described here apply in cases where the perpetrator has been correctly identified and both perpetrator and victim are tenants of the same landlord.

How to use this guide

Central to the approach in this book is the belief that most cases of racial harassment will ideally be resolved by stopping the harassment and maintaining the existing tenancies of both the victim and the perpetrator, not by moving one or the other, voluntarily or involuntarily. This belief is based partly on the well-documented slowness and difficulty of pursuing possession and other proceedings through the court. In 1991, London authorities identified 500 perpetrators, started proceedings against 68, and evicted eight.

The preparation, structure, conduct and follow-up for these interviews set out here is designed to convey to perpetrators that their behaviour may result in them losing their homes or being criminally prosecuted. They would therefore be well advised to desist from the harassment.

A secondary objective of the interview is the gaining of well-documented evidence which could be used in the event of legal proceedings. Detailed guidance on approaches to litigation is given in other publications listed in the bibliography.

The intention in writing this book is to offer straightforward practical guidance to assist staff and their managers who are keen to intervene early and tackle a problem that, if not attended to, can be complex and extremely distressing to the victims and to housing managers. The solutions on offer can also often seem far from practical.

Who is the guide for?

The guidance in this book may be used by:

— staff of local authority housing departments or housing associations who have not yet had experience of dealing with racial harassment but may be called upon to do so as part of their job

— staff who are currently handling cases, who may be feeling unsure and seeking guidance

— managers who do not themselves feel confident about the most effective way to handle interviews with perpetrators

— managers helping staff to prepare for interviews

— managers intervening in racial harassment cases, either to support the member of staff or to take over the case

— policy makers reviewing their organisation's approach to racial harassment and looking for suggestions of good practice.

CHAPTER 1

POLICY FRAMEWORK

Housing organisations which are keen to tackle racial harassment have adopted an approach broadly along the following lines:

Step 1   The report of the incident of racial harassment should be recorded by whichever member of staff receives it. This would not necessarily be someone in housing management. It may be a receptionist or a member of maintenance staff.

Step 2   Immediate maintenance work should be undertaken as necessary, e.g., removing graffiti, repairing windows, improving the security of property. This should be treated as emergency work and completed within 48 hours at the most.

Step 3   Housing management staff should interview the victim as soon as possible, definitely within 24 hours of the incident being reported.

— The details of the incident, including dates, times and witnesses should be recorded. The notes should be agreed with the victim.

— If a crime has been committed and the victim wishes to involve the police, they should be contacted immediately. Delay may prejudice the outcome of any criminal action.

— The organisation's policy and procedure should be explained to the victim.

— Options for action can then be discussed, including visiting and warning the perpetrator and increasing support to the victim. Supporting the victim and acting against the perpetrator should not be seen as alternatives. They should be acted on concurrently.

— It may take several visits to the victim before they have sufficient confidence in the organisation and trust in the individual housing manager to consent to a visit being made to the perpetrator or a report being made to the police.

— A course of action can then be agreed, summarised and noted. Some actions to support victims may involve other agencies such as helplines, law centres, victim support schemes, the police, and so on.

— Forms for the recording of any further incidents should be shown and explained to the victim. They should be available in the appropriate languages. The forms can then be left with the tenants for them to complete. — Interviewers should stress the need to report immediately any further incidents.

Step 4   The perpetrator can then be interviewed if the victim has consented.
This is covered in detail in chapter 3.

Step 5   A follow-up letter should be sent to the perpetrator confirming the discussion that took place, restating relevant clauses in the tenancy agreement and enclosing a copy of the organisation's policy.

Step 6   The victim should be kept informed of action taken and visited regularly, at least once a week, to ensure that harassment has not started again without being reported. Where regular visits are not possible frequent contact by telephone should be maintained.

Step 7   Further incidents of harassment might lead to more severe warnings being given to the perpetrator and ultimately criminal or civil proceedings, or possession proceedings under the tenancy agreement.

Step 8   Increased support should be provided to the victim as necessary. In some cases this might mean a temporary or permanent transfer.

Step 9   Repeated visits to the perpetrator should be made if harassment persists or recurs after a break.

Step 10   If harassment persists an investigation should be initiated with a view to legal proceedings being taken against the perpetrator.

Step 11   Appropriate action – criminal or civil, by landlord, police or victim – can be decided upon.

Step 12   Action against perpetrator.

Step 13   All incidents should be recorded and monitored centrally, not just on tenants' files. Regular reports on themes and issues, as well as overview statistics, should be regularly presented to relevant committees, at least annually.

Table 1: Policy framework for dealing with racial harassment

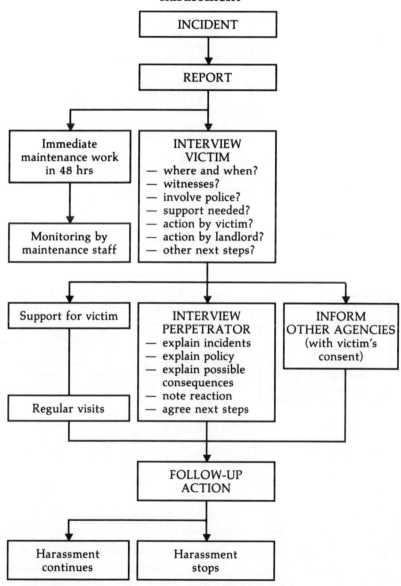

Table 2: Procedure if harassment continues after interview

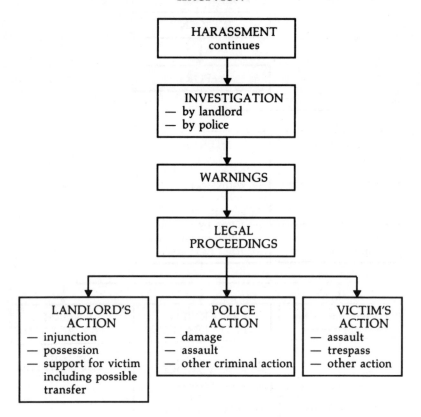

CHAPTER 2

COMMON REACTIONS

Working with victims

Victims have sometimes been reluctant to allow a landlord to visit perpetrators because of the fear of reprisals. Whilst this may be a justified first reaction, it is often possible to work with victims to build their confidence by offering them ongoing practical and emotional support. It may take several visits to secure the victim's agreement to the landlord's representative visiting the perpetrator.

In these circumstances, housing managers could be forgiven for feeling subconsciously or secretly relieved that they will not have to confront someone who is known for racist and aggressive behaviour. The housing manager might not therefore take all the steps available to reassure victims that they would be supported in the event of reprisals, and thus gain their consent to interviewing the perpetrator.

Black housing management staff who empathise strongly with the victims can, understandably, react particularly forcefully. They will fear that an encounter with the perpetrator could result in conflict, strong language, possibly even violence. There could also be a concern that their white managers will not take the problem as seriously as they do. These two factors may lead them to conclude that the best they can do is to do everything in their power to assist the victim, and not get involved with the perpetrator.

The result in these circumstances can often be that the only way for landlords to support victims is by transferring them. It is of course right that victims of racial harassment should be prioritised for transfers. An unwelcome by-product of this is, however, that the perpetrator succeeds in what they may well have been trying to achieve all along. The transfer of one victim may therefore encourage the perpetrator to behave in a similar way towards other potential victims of harassment.

Whilst the problem may be solved for one tenant, the cause of the problem remains latent and unsolved. There have also been cases of victims moving from one property only to confront racial harassment from a different perpetrator in their new home, so that even the limited objective of moving the victim away from the problem is not met.

Table 3 Summary of Support for Victim

- Undertake maintenance work immediately
- Improve security – locks, lighting, spy-holes, window reinforcement, etc
- Maintenance staff to monitor property regularly

- Arrange counselling, if necessary, through local victim support scheme, voluntary agency etc
- Escorts by relatives or friends to school, shops, etc
- Regular follow-up visits
- Take action against perpetrator after getting victim's consent
- Assist in getting legal advice
- Provide financial assistance for legal advice and taking action
- Investigate availability of temporary or permanent transfer
- Try and ensure after office hours support

Working with perpetrators

In the past, interviews with perpetrators have led to unseemly and unprofessional confrontations, sometimes even resulting in violence. Whilst there can be no excuse for violent behaviour, interviewers' behaviour may, intentionally or not, provoke perpetrators. On the other hand, appropriate behaviour by the interviewer can contribute to avoiding or preventing aggression or violence.

In order that interviews of perpetrators should lead to more productive outcomes, the people who are going to conduct the interview should meet with their line manager before the interview and consider how they are going to handle the various scenarios that might arise. It is not possible to predict the reactions of every perpetrator. There are, however, undoubtedly certain predictable patterns. Preparing for these will increase the interviewer's confidence. This in turn will assist interviewers in dealing with an unpredicted event or reaction.

Below, we list common reactions on the part of perpetrators. (Appropriate and inappropriate reactions to all these responses are set out in chapter 4).

Reaction 1 – Denial

Quote   'I don't know what you're talking about.'

_____

Reaction 2 – Blame someone else

Quote   'It was the kids. We didn't know they were doing it.'

Quote   'It was people off the estate.'

_____

Reaction 3 – Counter-accusation

Quote   'They've been harassing us. They started it. They call us names and fight with our kids.'

_____

Reaction 4 – Blame the victim

Quote   'They're always playing loud music.
             . . . having late night parties.
             . . . cooking smelly food.
             . . . dirtying the neighbourhood.

. . .   inviting all their relatives to come and
stay.
It's their fault.'

Reaction 5 – Shoot the messenger

Quote   'You people are always on the side of the
blacks. You can't come round here making
these accusations. I'm going to make a
complaint about you.'

Reaction 6 – Threatening behaviour

Quote   'I've had enough of your allegations – if
you don't get out I'll . . .'

CHAPTER 3

GUIDELINES FOR INTERVIEWERS

Purpose of the interview

The purpose of the initial interview is **NOT**:

— to accuse the perpetrator of the harassment
— to threaten them with imminent eviction
— to wring an admission of guilt from them
— to conduct a detective inquiry into what they did or did not do or say
— to convey the interviewer's sense of outrage at what the perpetrator has done and to tell them how angry racist behaviour makes the interviewer

The objectives of the interview are:

— to inform them that there has been a complaint
— to explain the organisation's policy and procedure on racial harassment

— by informing them of how seriously the organisation takes harassment and what the potential consequences are for them, discourage them from further abuse or attacks

Above all the purpose of the visit is to:

STOP THE HARASSMENT

Preparation for the interview

1   Perpetrators should not be interviewed by one person alone. Two people are necessary to provide support, ensure proper records are kept and as corroboration in the event of legal proceedings.

The lead interviewer should be the person primarily responsible for managing the tenancy of the victim, and therefore the one who will have interviewed the victim in detail about the incidents of harassment.

2   Interviewers should try to keep the interview impersonal. Direct accusations should be avoided. These are likely to make the person being interviewed angry and irrational.

3   An appointment should be made to see the tenant. It is best not to inform them when the appointment is made that the interview is about racial harassment. They should be told that the interview is to 'discuss their tenancy agreement'.

4   The interview will preferably be conducted in the office if the perpetrator is willing to come in. If not they will have to be visited in their home.

5   A copy of the policy and the relevant section of the tenancy agreement should be taken to the interview to be left with the tenants.

6   Line managers should note that black staff are likely to have stronger feelings than white staff because of their own experiences of racism, they are also likely to be treated differently by the perpetrator because they are black. Managers should affirm to black staff that their strong feelings are appropriate and are not a sign of weakness or lack of professionalism. Black staff can be assisted in managing these feelings so that they can continue to deal with perpetrators effectively without shying away or over-reacting.

   White staff may also have strong emotions about racial harassment which, if not managed, will affect the conduct of the interview. They may have a sense of outrage which will make them want to distance themselves from a white perpetrator. They may also feel ashamed or guilty at the behaviour of another white person. Managers should affirm that these reactions are understandable, and in many ways commendable, but that articulating these strong emotions, and making the perpetrator suitably remorseful, is not the purpose of the interview.

   Interviewers are unlikely to elicit an apology or a statement of remorse from the perpetrator. Therefore, trying to meet this personal objective may make interviewers feel frustrated or that the interview was a failure, when in fact the professional objective of conveying to the perpetrator the potential consequences of their behaviour, thus making them desist, may very well have been achieved.

There will also be staff who want to minimise the problem and question the motives of the victim (perhaps implying that the victim wants to 'jump the queue for a transfer'); or who believe that the incident is not racial harassment, but a neighbour dispute, or some other less serious matter. These staff should be reminded by line managers that the victim's perception is paramount. If they believe that the incident was racial harassment, then that should be the starting point for the organisation.

They should also be reminded of the policy and procedure of the organisation on racial harassment, compliance with which is not voluntary.

7   Interviewers should prepare themselves for how the interview is to be opened.

8   Before beginning, the interviewers should have discussed and agreed a clear structure for the interview with the help of the line manager, if necessary. They should also decide who is going to lead off during each stage.

Table 4: Structure of the Interview

Stage 1 Explanation of events

The designated interviewer should summarise key events, including information on dates, times and places, without making direct personal accusations or revealing who made the complaints.

Stage 2 Reactions of perpetrators

The interviewer should give the perpetrator time to react. If they do not say anything they should be asked for their comments on what they have heard.

Once the interviewer is sure they have understood the perpetrator's viewpoint they should note down their reactions. Detailed guidance on note-taking is given in the section below on behaviour in the interview.

Stage 3 Explanation of possible consequences

The organisation's policy should be summarised.

The relevant provisions in the tenancy agreement should be summarised, viz:

— the clause relating to harassment or nuisance

— the clause which says that the tenant is responsible for the behaviour of visitors or children.

Stage 4 Agreement of next steps

The next steps should be agreed, summarised and noted.

Table 5: Summary of Preparation

Interviews will go more smoothly and interviewers will have greater control if they make detailed preparations in the areas set out below.

- Name and address of alleged perpetrator
- Name and address of person(s) who identified them (to be kept confidential in the interview)
- Second person for the interview
- Date and time of interview
- Location
- Date of letter informing perpetrator of date, time and location of the interview
- Summary of incidents
- Opening remarks
- Explanation of reason for being there
- Descriptions of reported incidents
- Summary of clause in tenancy agreement
- Summary of the landlord's policy and procedure
- Summary of action the landlord might take
- Any other questions to ask perpetrator
- Description of follow-up action
- Ending the interview
- Closing remarks

Behaviour in the interview

1   Stick to the message. Interviewers should not be distracted down blind alleys.

2   If necessary calmly repeat what has been said as many times as required. This is called the 'broken

record' technique. Examples of this are given in chapter 4.

3   Use the authority of the tenancy agreement and the organisation's policies to prevent the interview turning into a one-to-one conflict. It will ensure that the perpetrator is reminded that the interviewer has the weight of the organisation behind them and is not acting out of personal animosity towards them.

4   Maintain the confidentiality of the victim by not revealing their name. Perpetrators are likely to try to elicit the names of whoever made the report, or they will form their own conclusions and seek to test them on the interviewer. In no circumstances, even where the perpetrator's guesses are accurate, should interviewers be drawn into these discussions.

5   Try not to get angry. When interviewers feel physical responses to anger or fear rising such as turning red, speaking too fast, sweaty palms, and so on, they should try to breathe deeply, slowly calming some of the physical reactions and managing the emotions of fear or anger. That will allow them to stick to the key messages and not be distracted into having a shouting match.

6   Support each other and intervene if one of the interviewers gets into difficulties. They should not be afraid to ask explicitly during the interview for the other interviewer to assist or to take over.

7   At the end of each stage of the interview, summarise and check back with the perpetrator about their

view of the situation, without commenting or passing judgment on what they have said.

8   Take notes of what is said. This should be done in as much detail as possible. The perpetrator's reactions should be recorded, preferably verbatim.

9   The interviewer who is not doing the talking should be responsible for taking notes. The two sets of notes can be combined afterwards.

10   Explain to the perpetrator that notes are being taken for the purposes of accurate record-keeping.

11   Show the notes to the perpetrators at the end of interview. They should be asked to sign them if they agree they are a true record of the discussion.

12   Leave a copy of the policy and the relevant clause in the tenancy agreement with the perpetrator. If they do not want to accept them, these documents can be included with the follow-up letter.

13   Interviewers should ensure they can see an unobstructed path to the exit if they need to leave in a hurry.

14   Decide in advance when and how to end the interview. This is helpful in ensuring that interviewers are working effectively in tandem.

Table 6: Summary of Behaviour in the Interview

- Conduct interview with a colleague
- Stick to the message
- Use the 'broken record' technique
- Use tenancy agreement and organisation's policy
- Maintain anonymity of victim
- Try not to get angry
- Breathe regularly and deeply to stay calm
- Summarise and reflect back what is being said
- Support each other
- Take notes
- Explain purpose of notes to perpetrator
- Show notes to perpetrator
- Leave copy of tenancy agreement and policy
- Decide in advance how the interview is to be ended
- Make sure there is no physical danger
- Make sure you can see your way to the exit

Following up the interview

1   If notes could not be taken during the interview they should be written up immediately afterwards. Contemporaneous notes may form a critical part of the evidence in the event of legal proceedings.

2   The interviewers should compare the notes they have taken and try to reach an agreed version of what was said.

3   The interview should be followed up in writing. Details on this are given in chapter 4.

4   Several visits and repeated warnings to perpetrators might be necessary. In many cases an initial visit may lead to a temporary abatement of the harassment. After some time the harassment might recur. It may not be appropriate in these circumstances to simply move on to legal proceedings. New warnings and reminders of previous ones will have to be given. If the pattern persists it might then be appropriate to take legal proceedings.

CHAPTER 4

CONDUCT OF THE INTERVIEW

In the previous chapters, different reactions from perpetrators have been highlighted as well as general approaches to the interview. This chapter focuses on the actual words that interviewers might use. It provides a script of appropriate language and identifies common and possibly damaging approaches. The script avoids aggressive, personal attacks which might be interpreted by the perpetrator as persecuting them. It emphasises clear, simple explanation, repeated if necessary. It is designed to convey the four key messages set out below.

Table 7: Key Messages given to the Perpetrator
1 The organisation takes racial harassment very seriously.
2 Racial harassment is a breach of the tenancy agreement.
3 Racial harassment could result in possession of the property being sought.
4 The harassment must stop.

Introductions

Don't say   'Hello. We've come to talk about the racial harassment you've been committing against Mrs Brown.'

Do say   'Hello. We've come to talk about breaches of our tenancy agreement by some of our tenants in this area.'

Beginning the interview

Don't say   'We have had a report that you have been racially harassing Mr Khan.'

Do say   'I'm visiting to inform you that we have had reports of incidents of racial harassment in this area. The organisation takes racial harassment very seriously and we are keen to do everything we can to stamp it out.'

'I would like to explain our policy on racial harassment to you.'

Explaining the incidents

Don't say   'You have been seen . . .

. . . shouting at them in the street

. . . delivering anonymous letters

. . . emptying rubbish outside their front door

. . . breaking their windows

. . . kicking their door in.'

Do say   'One of our tenants in this area . . .

. . . has been called names in the street

. . . received anonymous letters

. . . had rubbish emptied outside their front door

. . . had their windows broken

. . . had their door kicked in.'

Don't say   'You called them pakis and wogs.'

Do say   'Asian tenants of ours in this area have been called names and racially abused on various occasions.'

Don't say   'Your kids called them racist names.'

Do say   'Local kids have been heard calling them racist names.'

Don't say   'You were seen delivering anonymous, abusive notes.'

Do say   'They have been receiving letters containing racial abuse.'

Don't say   'Friends of yours attacked them in the street.'

Do say 'They have been attacked in the street. This may have been by people who are not tenants of ours but they might know our tenants.'

Perpetrator seeks more information

Perpetrator 'Who's making these accusations? I bet it's . . .'

Don't say 'Yes, it is.'

Do say 'We investigate all complaints that are made to us. Any tenant who makes a complaint has a right to their confidentiality being respected.'

Perpetrator 'Are they accusing us then?'

Don't say 'Yes, they are.'

Do say 'The policy of the organisation is that we will not tolerate racial harassment and so we investigate all complaints.'

Perpetrator 'What evidence have you got that we did it?'

Don't say 'I'm not willing to disclose that, but we do have evidence.'

Do say 'We investigate all complaints of racial harassment and where they are proven we will take action.'

Perpetrator	'So you haven't got any proof.'
Don't say	'Yes we have, but I'm not prepared to tell you what it is.'
Or	'No we haven't, but we will get some.'
Do say	'As I have already said, we investigate all cases of racial harassment and where they are proven, we will take action.'

Perpetrator	'What sort of action?'
Don't say	'We will evict anyone caught racially harassing one of our tenants.'
Do say	'The organisation's tenancy agreement says that if tenants persist in racial harassment and do not heed warnings the landlord can treat this as a ground for possession. I have a copy of the agreement here. Would you like to have a look?'

Perpetrator's reactions

| **Don't say** | 'Have you got anything to say about your harassment of Mr Khan's family? I'll need to take notes of what you say in case of a court case.' |
| **Do say** | 'Before we get on to discussing the tenancy agreement in detail, have you got any comments on the incidents I have told you about? I hope you don't mind me |

taking notes. It is so that we have an accurate record of the interview.'

It is important to remember that the 'broken record' technique – repeating the same simple message – can often be effective in moving the conversation on and preventing the confrontation escalating into accusations and counter-accusations.

Reaction 1 – Denial

Perpetrator   'I haven't done anything. You can't come round to our house accusing us of harassing people. I don't know what you're talking about.'

Don't say   'We have information that on 21 January you were seen in the street shouting racist abuse. You were also seen running away from Mr Wong's flat after fireworks had been put through the letter box.'

Do say   'Incidents have taken place such as . . .

. . . tenants being racially abused in the street

. . . having fireworks put though their letter box.

We take racial harassment very seriously so we ask our tenants to sign a tenancy agreement which says that racial harassment is breach of the agreement and could result in the landlord seeking possession of the property. Have you got any comments on any of these incidents?'

Perpetrator   'Are you saying that you're going to evict us without any proof?'

Don't say   'If the harassment continues, we will serve notice of seeking possession on you.'

Do say   'As I mentioned the policy of the organisation is that we want to stop racial harassment and we would consider seeking possession against anyone who continued to do it after being warned.'

Reaction 2 – Blame someone else

Perpetrator   'There is some harassment around here, but it's caused by other people, not people who live around here.'

Don't say   'Our information is that you are involved, even though there might be others involved.'

Do say   'We investigate all complaints and visit everyone who might be involved to explain our policy to them. We take racial harassment very seriously and are determined to do all we can to stamp it out and to help people who are being harassed.
                   We also explain that tenants are

responsible under their tenancy agreement for the behaviour of all members of
their household and their visitors.'

Reaction 2a - Blame children

Perpetrator   'It's local kids. They're always causing
trouble. Mine get involved, but it's
because others are leading them into
trouble. There's nothing I can do about it.
I can't control them if I'm not around.'

Don't say   'We know it's your kids and you have to
control them.'

Do say   'Under the tenancy agreement the tenant
is responsible for ensuring that their
children and their visitors do not cause a
nuisance to or harass other tenants.'

Reaction 3 - Counter-accusation

Perpetrator   'I don't know about us harassing them.
They've been harassing us - with their
loud music and parties, friends coming
round all hours of the day and night,
smelly food, relatives coming and staying
and overcrowding the place. Do you
know how many people they've got living
there?'

Don't say   'How many people they've got living
there is nothing to do with you. All the
other things you're accusing them of are

what people always accuse black people of. They're just ignorance and prejudice.'

Do say   'We investigate all complaints that are made, whoever they come from. I'm here to investigate the complaints we have already had, and to tell you about the organisation's policy on racial harassment.

If you would like to make a separate complaint, that will also be investigated. At the moment I want to concentrate on the incidents that have already taken place and confirm what your tenancy agreement says and what our policy is.'

It is important that if perpetrators make counter-accusations, the same reporting procedure should be followed; however it is advisable that someone else investigates these complaints separately. If the same housing manager is dealing with both sets of complaints, relationships become very confused and the trust necessary for effectively supporting the victim is undermined.

Reaction 4 – Blame the victim

Perpetrator   'This area used to be so nice before they moved in.

. . . Ever since their kind came the place is filthy.

. . . They won't mix.

. . . They're unfriendly.

. . . They've taken over the school.

. . . That's why all these things are happening to them. They deserve all they get. They should leave this area or put up with it. It's no good them complaining about us.'

Don't say   'No wonder they won't mix if they have to deal with attitudes like yours. This area hasn't got dirtier since they moved in. You're just prejudiced.

We are not going to allow no-go areas for black people.'

Do say   'Our policy is that people should be allocated housing according to their needs, not according to areas. We cannot preserve any areas for a particular group.

In our view there are no acceptable justifications for harassment and we are committed to stopping it. If necessary we will take legal action against proven perpetrators, as I have already said.'

It is vital that interviewers should not be distracted into challenging every racial prejudice that is expressed. They should try to stick to their key messages.

Reaction 5 – Shoot the messenger

Perpetrator   'You people are always on the side of the blacks. It's all gone the other way.'

Don't say   'That's because there are so many racists

around and it's mainly black people that are harassed.'

Do say 'Our policy applies equally to everybody, regardless of colour and race. I am going to leave a copy of the policy with you.'

Reaction 6 – Threatening behaviour

Perpetrator 'I've had enough of your allegations. If you don't watch out I'll . . .'

Don't say 'You'd better not or I'll . . .'

Do say 'I will have to end the interview if you are going to threaten me.'

Whenever there is any danger of physical violence the interviewers must leave as quickly as possible, but without running or looking as though they are panicking.

Ending the interview

The interviewers need to assure themselves that the perpetrator has received the key messages. They should then check that they and the perpetrator are satisfied with their notes and there is nothing that needs further clarification or discussion.

The interviewer can then summarise the next steps that everybody has agreed on, checking these with their colleague and the perpetrator. If nothing has been agreed, the interview should be ended by the interviewers summarising their point of view and that of the perpetrators.

Leave a copy of the organisation's policy on racial harassment and a copy of the relevant section of the tenancy agreement.

If nothing else is going to be agreed by more discussion, the interviewers should say goodbye and depart.

Follow-up after the interview

After the interview, discuss what happened as soon as possible with a line manager or a colleague. Interviewers should be encouraged to talk about:

— what was discussed
— how they felt about it
— what decisions need to be taken
— which other agencies need to be informed
— what records are necessary for the file and for monitoring purposes
— what are the other next steps
— who is responsible for enacting each of the next steps
— time scales for the next steps
— contingency plans if the harassment continues or recurs

It will be helpful for interviewers to discuss how they felt, as well as what happened. Bottling up feelings of fear, frustration, powerlessness, anger or resentment – many of these feelings being a reflection of the victim's feelings – will affect how objective the housing manager will be able to be in dealings with both the victim and the perpetrator in future.

The perpetrator can then be written to confirming the discussion that took place and any conclusions that were reached. The letter can also outline the next steps to be taken.

Table 8: Following up the Interview

- Write confirming discussion and outlining next steps
- Visit victim and report back on interview with perpetrator
- Arrange any further support needed by victim
- Record discussions and decisions on victim's, perpetrator's and central racial harassment file
- Fill in monitoring forms
- Inform any other relevant agencies

CHAPTER 5

CHALLENGING DISCRIMINATORY BEHAVIOUR

In dealing effectively with racial harassment, housing staff need to have a more general sense of appropriate responses and approaches to challenging discriminatory behaviour. Without this they may feel powerless and paralysed when confronted with abusive remarks or hostile behaviour.

Many people are concerned that challenging discriminatory language or behaviour will always result in conflict and that therefore the best response is either to ignore the behaviour, to joke about it or literally to walk away altogether.

Unfortunately, most people with prejudices will assume, if the person they are talking to remains silent, that they share the prejudice, and so will be encouraged to continue with the behaviour. A joke is often too subtle a challenge, the point of which is often lost on the other person. Walking away from the situation leaves the other person with no indication of what kind of behaviour is expected from them in the future. So, instead of them changing their behaviour, the relationship between the two people is likely to become permanently estranged. In the future, they will have difficulty maintaining normal, open communication.

There are some simple rules for effectively challenging discriminatory behaviour.

Table 9: Challenging Discriminatory Behaviour

1   Talk about 'I' not 'You'. For example 'I find your jokes offensive and not very funny' instead of: 'You are racist.'

2   Challenge, do not confront.

3   Focus on behaviour, not character, as in the example given above.

4   Do not try to change people's prejudices, just their behaviour.

5   Do not expect the other person to agree with you. Just make sure they have heard what you have said.

6   Go back to people afterwards if you cannot think of the most effective way to challenge them at the time.

7   Ask for other people's support either in assisting you to decide on how to challenge the behaviour, or in joining the challenge.

CHAPTER 6

INTERVIEWS PRECEDING LEGAL ACTION

The interview described in chapter 4 is designed for early intervention following reported incidents of racial harassment. As has already been acknowledged, the harassment may persist notwithstanding the informal warnings that have been given. It will then be necessary to consider initiating legal proceedings, i.e., issuing formal warnings and notices of the landlord's intentions. The landlord may consider seeking an injunction not to cause a nuisance, or seek a suspended or immediate possession order. Before issuing such notices or warnings, housing managers must conduct a thorough investigation.

The form of the interview with both victim and perpetrator that is undertaken before legal proceedings will depend on the nature of the proposed action. Housing managers will also need to have expert legal advice before embarking on legal proceedings. This guide is not intended to cover all such interviews as they are more appropriately dealt with in a discussion of approaches to legal remedies. However, a few simple considerations should be mentioned here, together with principles that apply in all cases.

In the first instance, in order to instigate legal proceedings it will be necessary for victims to record accurately and regularly the date, time, place and exact nature of all incidents that take place, as well as the names and address of witnesses.

Following this, witnesses will have to be interviewed and asked to record their recollection of events as precisely as possible. They will also have to be asked to indicate their willingness to give evidence in court, sign a written statement, or at least be interviewed by the police.

It may also be the case that there are other people who have been subjected to racial harassment by the same perpetrators. If so, they will also have to be interviewed and their experiences recorded in a form that can be used in the event of legal proceedings.

The collection of this evidence will be crucial to the success of any legal action. It is important to act as expeditiously as possible to save the victim from further harassment, but it is also essential to be thorough in preparing the case.

Once this evidence has been gathered, although it is necessary to keep the evidence and the identity of the witnesses confidential, the incidents described should be discussed with the perpetrator, together with a recap of previous visits, interviews or discussions in which they have been asked to stop the harassment. The perpetrator should be asked for their comments. If they deny involvement with any or all of the incidents when strong evidence exists of their participation in the harassment, they will have to be served with formal notice of the landlord's intention to act.

They may acknowledge their complicity in the harassment. In these circumstances they should be asked to give a written undertaking of their willingness not to engage in any further harassment or hostility, and to ensure those for whom they are responsible, for example, their children or visitors, also desist from hostility. If the undertaking is then broken, formal action will have to be initiated.

CHAPTER 7

OTHER NECESSARY ACTION

The approach set out in this book deals with one aspect of the problem of racial harassment – interviewing perpetrators. In order to deal effectively with a problem that has in the past not been attacked with a vigour in proportion to the endurance or suffering of the victims, local authorities and housing organisations will need other strategies in place. These will include:

1   Ensuring that tenants who are suffering racial harassment report the incidents and have confidence in the willingness and the ability of landlords to do something about it.

2   Publicising the policy of the organisation on racial harassment to all tenants.

3   Continuing support for victims other than transferring them, which may not be possible or desirable.

4   Supporting victims where the perpetrators have not been identified. Where crimes have been com-

mitted, landlords will have to work closely with the police to identify and deter perpetrators.

5   Supporting and building the confidence of victims who have identified perpetrators but do not want the landlord to interview for fear of reprisals, or for any other reason.

6   Dealing with perpetrators who are not tenants of the same landlord. Effective joint working with other agencies such as other landlords, the police and community organisations will be necessary here, not just in order to take criminal proceedings, but also to deter perpetrators in the early stages.

7   Dealing with perpetrators who are themselves vulnerable and with whom it will be difficult to apply the normal deterrents and sanctions. These cases are hard to generalise about and will have to be treated on their individual merits; nonetheless, the vulnerability of the perpetrator should not be used to obscure or ignore the needs of the victim.

8   Where all methods of deterrence fail, housing organisations must be sure that they are equipped to use the power of the courts to assist victims and take legal action against perpetrators. This will mean that staff will need knowledge and skills in:

   — possession proceedings

   — seeking and enforcing different forms of injunctions

   — what constitutes criminal damage and assault

- the availability of criminal injuries compensation

- methods of gathering and recording evidence

- sources of specialist legal advice which may not be available within the organisation or from their usual legal advisers.

Placing too much emphasis on one particular strategy, for example, moving victims or evicting perpetrators, will result in the problem persisting outside the compass of rigid bureaucratic structures which are, in the case of racial harassment, as with everything else, inimical to meeting the needs of vulnerable people.

INTERVIEW PROFORMAS

These proformas are designed to assist housing managers in focusing on what they need to do before and after interviews of perpetrators. They should be used as *aides-mémoire* and checklists. There are four in all:

1 Preparation for the interview
2 Prompt for the interview
3 Record of perpetrator's responses
4 Follow-up action

They are not substitutes for other forms of record keeping and monitoring. They are tools for the interviewers.

The lead interviewer, i.e., the person with primary responsibility for managing the tenancy of the victim, should fill them in and give copies to their co-interviewers and their line managers. They should also be kept on victim's and perpetrator's files, as well as on a central racial harassment file for monitoring purposes.

On pages 70–86, we provide examples of completed interview proformas.

INTERVIEWING PERPETRATORS OF RACIAL HARASSMENT

Interview proforma 1

Preparation for the interview

CONFIDENTIAL

To be filled in before the interview by the housing officer responsible for the patch on which the victim lives.

NB This form should not be shown, or seen by accident, by the perpetrator. If interviewers want to take information off it to help as a prompt at the interview, they should use proforma 4

Name of housing officer: _____

_____

Date form completed: _____

_____

Name and address of alleged perpetrator: _____

_____

_____

_____

_____

_____

Name and address of person(s) who identified them (if they were not the victim, note their relationship to the victim):

1. _____

Victim/Witness (delete as applicable)

2. _____

_____

_____

_____

Victim/Witness (delete as applicable)

3. _____

_____

_____

_____

Victim/Witness (delete as applicable)

Second person to attend the interview _____

_____

Date and time of interview _____

_____

Location _____

Date of letter informing perpetrator of date, time and location of the interview _____

_____

_____

_____

Summary of incidents

Description of incident _____

_____

_____

_____

_____

_____

_____

_____

_____

_____

_____

_____

_____

_____

_____

_____

_____

_____

Date _____

Time _____

Place _____

Name and address of witness _____

_____

_____

Opening Remarks

Who is going to open the interview? _____

_____

Introductions: _____

_____

_____

_____

_____

_____

Reason for being there: _____

_____

_____

_____

_____

_____

Descriptions of the incidents that have been reported: _____

_____

_____

_____

_____

_____

_____

_____

_____

_____

Summary of clause in tenancy agreement: _____

_____

_____

_____

_____

_____

_____

_____

Summary of the landlord's policy and procedure:

_____

_____

_____

_____

_____

_____

Summary of what action the landlord might take:

_____

_____

_____

_____

_____

_____

_____

_____

Any other questions to ask perpetrator _____

_____

_____

_____

_____

_____

_____

_____

_____

_____

At the end of the interview how are you going to communicate to each other that you think the interview should be terminated? _____

_____

Ending the interview

Description of follow-up action _____

_____

_____

_____

_____

Closing remarks _____

_____

_____

_____

_____

* *For a completed example of proforma 1, see p 70.*

INTERVIEWING PERPETRATORS OF RACIAL HARASSMENT

Interview proforma 2

Prompt for the interview

CONFIDENTIAL

To be completed in advance by the two interviewers and to be taken to the interview. Both interviewers should have a copy.

Name of housing officer: _____

Date form completed: _____

Checklist:
Three copies of the following documents needed – for both interviewers and one to be left with the perpetrator:

— Relevant clause in tenancy agreement

— Racial harassment policy

— Racial harassment procedure

Interview:

Introductions: _____

_____

_____

_____

_____

_____

Reason for being there: _____

_____

_____

_____

_____

_____

Descriptions of the incidents that have been reported: _____

_____

_____

_____

_____

_____

_____

Summary of clause in tenancy agreement: _____

_____

_____

_____

_____

_____

_____

Summary of the landlord's policy and procedure:

_____

_____

_____

_____

_____

Summary of what action the landlord might take:

_____
_____
_____
_____
_____
_____
_____
_____

At the end of the interview how are you going to communicate to each other that you think the interview should be terminated? _____

_____
_____

What are you going to say to end the interview?

_____
_____
_____
_____

For a completed example of proforma 2, see p 77.

INTERVIEWING PERPETRATORS OF RACIAL HARASSMENT

Interview proforma 3

Record of perpetrator's responses

CONFIDENTIAL

These should be recorded by the person accompanying the interviewer. The notes should reflect as exactly as possible what the perpetrator says, not judgments about it made by the person taking the notes.

Agreed questions can be entered on the proforma in advance.

Name of housing officer: _____

Date form completed: _____

Perpetrator's responses in detail

Immediate response: _____
_____
_____
_____
_____
_____
_____
_____

Answers to specific questions:

Question 1 _____

_____

Answer _____

_____

_____

Question 2 _____

_____

Answer _____

_____

_____

Question 3 _____

_____

_____

Answer _____

_____

Question 4 _____

_____

_____

_____

Answer _____

_____

_____

Question 5 _____

_____

Answer _____

_____

_____

_____

Question 6 _____

Answer _____

_____

_____

_____

Question 7 _____

Answer _____

_____

_____

_____

Question 8 _____

Answer _____

_____

_____

_____

Any other responses _____

_____

_____

_____

_____

_____

_____

_____

Date and time when notes made _____

_____

_____

Place where notes made _____

_____

_____

Name of notetaker _____

Job title _____

Signature _____

For a completed example of proforma 3, see p 80.

INTERVIEWING PERPETRATORS OF RACIAL HARASSMENT

Interview proforma 4

Follow-up action

CONFIDENTIAL

To be filled in by housing officer.

Name of housing officer _____

Date form completed _____

Has the perpetrator been written to summarising the discussion and re-stating any agreed next steps? _____

Date of letter _____

Have copies of the letter gone to the perpetrator's file, the victim's file and the central racial harassment file? _____

_____

_____

Have the necessary monitoring forms been filled in and circulated? _____

Has the case been discussed with your line manager? _____

_____

_____

_____

What further actions are needed? _____

_____

_____

_____

_____

_____

_____

_____

Which other agencies need to be informed? _____

_____

_____

_____

_____

Dates they are to be/have been informed: _____

_____

_____

_____

_____

Have copies of letter(s) to other agencies or notes
of meeting gone to the victim's and the perpetrator's file? _____

_____

What feedback is to be given to the victim? ___

_____

_____

_____

_____

What measures need to be taken to protect the victim from any reprisals? _____

_____

_____

_____

_____

_____

_____

_____

_____

_____

_____

_____

_____

_____

_____

_____

* For a completed example of proforma 4, see p 84.

INTERVIEWING PERPETRATORS OF RACIAL HARASSMENT

Interview proforma 1

Preparation for the interview

CONFIDENTIAL

To be filled in before the interview by the housing officer responsible for the patch on which the victim lives.

NB This form should not be shown, or seen by accident, by the perpetrator. If interviewers want to take information off it to help as a prompt at the interview, they should use proforma 4

Name of housing officer: _____

John Robinson

Date form completed: _____

_1/12/93_

Name and address of alleged perpetrator: _____

16-year-old son, Barry, of
Mr & Mrs Wilson, 64 Square Street
and 3 of his school friends.
Names not known, nor whether
they are our tenants.

Name and address of person(s) who identified them (if they were not the victim, note their relationship to the victim):

1. _Mrs. Patel , 42 Square Street_

Victim/~~Witness~~ (delete as applicable)

2. _Mr. & Mrs. Patel's two children who were present when the window was broken. Also called names in the street by Barry Wilson and his mates._

Victim/~~Witness~~ (delete as applicable)

3. _Mrs. Amin, not our tenant. A friend of Mrs. Patel's who was present when a brick came through window. Mrs. Amin's address , 22 Circle Street_

~~Victim~~/Witness (delete as applicable)

Second person to attend the interview _____

Mary Marsh , Senior Housing Officer

Date and time of interview _____

_4/12/93 - 3.00 p.m._

Location _Head Office_

Date of letter informing perpetrator of date, time and location of the interview _27/11/93_

-registered post. I telephoned & they said they would be coming to the interview. Father & mother will attend.

Summary of incidents

Description of incident _____

Brick thrown through window

Date _10/11/93_

Time _4.00 p.m._

Place _Mr. & Mrs. Patel's house, 42 Square St._

Name and address of witness _____

Mrs. Amin, 22 Circle St.

Summary of incidents

Description of incident _____

Name calling of Mr. & Mrs.
Patel's children
'Pakis piss off home'
'Wogs out'

Date _12/11/93 & other previous occasions_
Time _8.45 a.m._
Place _Corner of Circle & Square St._

Name and address of witness _____

Opening Remarks

Who is going to open the interview? _____

John Robinson

Introductions: _My name is John Robinson. I'm your housing officer. This is my colleague, Mary Marsh. She is a senior housing officer. I don't think you have met either of us before._

Reason for being there: _A number of incidents have taken place involving abuse and attacks on the property of one of our tenants in this area. We thought it would be useful to visit other tenants in the area._

Descriptions of the incidents that have been reported: _The children of one of our Asian tenants have repeatedly been called names in the street. Now the same family have had a brick thrown through their window by local youths. Some of them have been recognised as children of our tenants._

Summary of clause in tenancy agreement: _____

You might remember that when you
signed the tenancy agreement we
pointed out various clauses to you.
One of them was that we
regarded racial harassment as
unacceptable nuisance to our
other tenants. I have a copy here.

Summary of the landlord's policy and procedure:

We also have a policy which
explains that we want to do
everything possible to stop
racial harassment. We therefore
visit other tenants in the area
and explain our policy.

Summary of what action the landlord might take:

Where the people doing the
harassment are identified, we
warn them and ask them to stop.
If the harassment continues,
we will take stronger action,
involving the police and in extreme
cases, seeking possession of
the home of the person doing
the harassment.

Any other questions to ask perpetrator _____

1. Have you heard anything about incidents in this area?
2. Can you tell us anything about them?
3. Did you know about the clause in our tenancy agreement and our policy?
4. Did you realise that the holders of the tenancy were responsible for the behaviour of others who live in the house?

At the end of the interview how are you going to communicate to each other that you think the interview should be terminated? _____

Start packing up papers

Ending the interview

Description of follow-up action _____

I will write to you confirming our discussions. I'm leaving a copy of the tenancy agreement and the policy with you.

Closing remarks _____ Thanks for coming in. I hope you're clear about our policy now. If there are any other problems, or if you have any problems we'll see you again.

INTERVIEWING PERPETRATORS OF RACIAL HARASSMENT

Interview proforma 2

Prompt for the interview

CONFIDENTIAL

To be completed in advance by the two inter-viewers and to be taken to the interview. Both interviewers should have a copy.

Name of housing officer: _John Robinson_

Date form completed: _1/12/93_

Checklist:

Three copies of the following documents needed - for both interviewers and one to be left with the perpetrator:

— Relevant clause in tenancy agreement
— Racial harassment policy
— Racial harassment procedure

Interview:

Introductions: _My name is John Robinson. I'm your housing officer. This is my colleague, Mary Marsh. She is a senior housing officer. I don't think you have met either of us before._

Reason for being there: A number of incidents have taken place involving abuse and attacks on the property of one of our tenants in this area. we thought it would be useful to visit other tenants in the area.

Descriptions of the incidents that have been reported: The children of one of our Asian tenants have repeatedly been called names in the street. Now the same family have had a brick thrown through their window by local youths. Some of them have been recognised as children of our tenants.

Summary of clause in tenancy agreement: You might remember that when you signed the tenancy agreement we pointed out various clauses to you. One of them was that we regarded racial harassment as unacceptable nuisance to our other tenants. I have a copy here.

Summary of the landlord's policy and procedure: We also have a policy which explains that we want to do everything possible to stop racial harassment. We therefore visit other tenants in the area and explain our policy.

Summary of what action the landlord might take:

Where the people doing the harassment are identified, we warn them and ask them to stop. If the harassment continues, we will take stronger action, involving the police and in extreme cases, seeking possession of the home of the person doing the harassment.

At the end of the interview how are you going to communicate to each other that you think the interview should be terminated? _____

Start packing up papers.

What are you going to say to end the interview?

Thanks for coming in. I hope you're clear about our policy now. If there are any other problems, or if you have any problems we'll see you again.

INTERVIEWING PERPETRATORS OF RACIAL HARASSMENT

Interview proforma 3

Record of perpetrator's responses

CONFIDENTIAL

These should be recorded by the person accompanying the interviewer. The notes should reflect as exactly as possible what the perpetrator says, not judgments about it made by the person taking the notes.

Agreed questions can be entered on the proforma in advance.

Name of housing officer: _John Robinson_

Date form completed: _4/12/93_

Perpetrator's responses in detail

Immediate response: _____

They didn't know anything about these incidents. They couldn't control their son. They would speak to him. Although they were sure he wasn't involved in anything like this, they would warn him anyway.

Answers to specific questions:

Question 1 _Have you heard anything about incidents in this area?_

Answer _No, but there were some rough boys who their son had made friends with at school._

Question 2 _Can you tell us anything more about the incidents we described?_

Answer _No_

Question 3 _Did you know about the clause in our tenancy agreement & our policy on racial harassment?_

Answer _No_

Question 4 _Did you realise that the holders of the tenancy were responsible for the behaviour of others who lived in the property?_

Answer _No. But they would speak to their son and tell him to stay out of these things._

Question 5 _Do you know anyone else who might be involved?_

Answer _Joe Samuels, Bob Roberts, Winston Green. All boys at Admiral Crichton school with their son. Some were his friends and they were the sort of boys that might be involved._

Question 6 _____

Answer _____
_____
_____
_____

Question 7 _____

Answer _____
_____
_____
_____

Question 8 _____

Answer _____
_____
_____
_____

Any other responses _Asked if we were going to evict them. Our response: "Our policy is that if tenants, or anyone in their house, continued harassing other tenants by abusing them or attacking their property after they had been warned we would seek possession._

Date and time when notes made _____
_4/12/93_
_5.00 p.m._

Place where notes made _____
Head office

Name of notetaker _Mary Marsh_
Job title _Senior Housing Officer_

Signature _Mary Marsh_

INTERVIEWING PERPETRATORS OF RACIAL HARASSMENT

Interview proforma 4

Follow-up action

CONFIDENTIAL

To be filled in by housing officer.

Name of housing officer _John Robinson_

Date form completed _5/12/93_

Has the perpetrator been written to summarising the discussion and re-stating any agreed next steps? _Yes_

Date of letter _5/12/93_

Have copies of the letter gone to the perpetrator's file, the victim's file and the central racial harassment file? _Yes_

Have the necessary monitoring forms been filled in and circulated? _Yes_

Has the case been discussed with your line manager? _Yes_

What further actions are needed? _____

1. To visit headmaster of Admiral Crichton School.

2. To contact police about broken window.

3. To visit Mrs. Patel to make sure that there have been no further incidents.

Which other agencies need to be informed? ____

1. Police

2. School

Dates they are to be/have been informed: ____

Appointment with school 11/12/93
Police contacted 5/12/93

Have copies of letter(s) to other agencies or notes of meeting gone to the victim's and the perpetrator's file? ___Yes_____

What feedback is to be given to the victim? ___

Appointment arranged for 7/12/93

What measures need to be taken to protect the victim from any reprisals? _____

1. Increased security.
Maintenance to inspect.
2. Mrs. Amin, the friend at
22 Circle Street, to be visited
and asked to accompany
Mrs. Patel in taking the
children to school.

BIBLIOGRAPHY

Brown, C *Black and White Britain: the third PSI survey*, Heinemann, 1984.

Commission for Racial Equality *Living in Terror: a report on racial violence and harassment in housing*, 1987.

Commission for Racial Equality *Code of Practice in Rented Housing*, 1991.

Community and Race Relations Unit, British Council of Churches *Racist Attacks: a call for Christian action*, 1987.

Forbes, D *Action on Racial Harassment*, Legal Action Group, 1988.

Forman, C 'No Let Up in Racist Violence', *Black Housing*, December 1992.

Gordon, P *Racial Violence and Harassment*, Runnymede Trust, 1986.

Greater London Council *Racial Harassment in London: report of a panel of inquiry*, 1984.

Greater London Council and Racial Harassment Bill Group *Racial Harassment – Time to Act: report of a conference*, 1986.

Home Affairs Committee *Racial Attacks and Harassment* (HC 409), HMSO, 1986.

Home Department, Secretary of State for *Racial Attacks and Harassment: government reply to the third report from the Home Affairs Committee* (CM 45), HMSO, 1986.

Hounslow, London Borough of *The Nature and Extent of Racial Harassment in the London Borough of Hounslow*, 1985.

Independent Commission of Inquiry into Racial Harassment *Racial Harassment in Leeds 1985–6*, Leeds Community Relations Council, 1987.

Kelly, D and Rosewarne, A: *Tenants Tackle Racism: an account of a series of experimental workshops held in Stepney 1984–5*, Dame Colet House, Limehouse Field Tenants Association and Tower Hamlets Tenants Federation, 1986.

Legal Action Group *Making the Law Work Against Racial Harassment*, 1990.

Local Authority Housing and Racial Equality Working Party *Racial Harassment: a strategy for racial equality in housing – a policy and good practice guide for local authorities*, Association of Metropolitan Authorities, 1987.

London Race and Housing Forum *Racial Harassment on Local Authority Housing Estates*, Commission for Racial Equality, 1980.

Manchester Council for Community Relations *Racial Harassment in Manchester and the Response of the Police 1980–5*, 1986.

Merseyside Action Against Racial Terrorism *Racial Terrorism in Merseyside*, Merseyside Community Relations Council, 1987.

Metropolitan Police *Racial Harassment Action Guide*, 1987.

National Federation of Housing Associations *Racial Harassment, Policies and Procedures for Housing Associations*, 1989.

Redbridge Community Relations Council *Silence Gives Consent: racist attacks in Redbridge – what is to be done?*, 1986.

Searchlight *The Murderers are Among Us: the criminal records of Britain's racists*, 1985.

Walsh, D *Racial Harassment in Glasgow*, Scottish Ethnic Minorities Research Unit, 1987.

LEMOS ASSOCIATES BOOKS

Lemos Associates aims to assist organisations in achieving equality of opportunity. We believe that unless organisations include equality perspectives in almost all areas of their work they will not be as efficient or effective, as well as not being as fair, as they could. The areas affected by equal opportunities include: recruitment and selection, harassment at work, career development, appraisal, training, managing a diverse workforce, performance management, childcare support, equality in service delivery, and reaching the widest markets for goods and services.

With regard to housing, the consideration of equal opportunities will have an impact on access and allocations of housing: type, location and quality, service delivery and harassment.

Our books are published to provide:

1   Information to managers, human resources and housing professionals as well as others committed to equality of opportunity.

2   Advice and information on formulating strategies, policies and procedures.

3   Practical, easy-to-implement guidance and assistance on handling cases of individuals who feel they are being discriminated against.

4   Practical, easy-to-implement guidance and assistance on handling those who the manager, or others in the organisation, believe are behaving in a discriminatory manner.

OTHER TITLES
IN THE SERIES

Interviewing Perpetrators of Racial Harassment is one of a series of guides for housing managers. Those in preparation include:

Policies and Procedures for Dealing with Racial Harassment

This book, to be published in 1993, will review current best practice in devising and implementing policies and procedures for dealing with racial harassment.

Supporting Victims of Racial Harassment

Also to be published in 1993, this book will advise on how to give practical and emotional support to victims of racial harassment so that they feel less vulnerable and are able to participate in stopping the harassment with the support of the landlord.

Legal Remedies for Dealing with Racial Harassment

Currently in preparation, this book will give practical guidance for housing managers on what legal provisions, such as possession, injunctions, and criminal proceedings can be used in cases of racial harassment, and how to go about using those remedies.

Case Studies on Dealing with Racial Harassment

A review of previous cases of racial harassment, how they are handled by local authorities and housing associations, and what the outcomes were.